MW01283727

Stand-up 6:
The Heckler's Bit

ISBN-13: 978-1984204271

Printed in the United States of America

"I was looking up quotes about *heckling;* I couldn't find any good ones, *nothing* clever. One guy said something about hecklers not having the courage to say it to their face, and how they were *cowardly* for yelling it out *anonymously* from the back of a darkened room. This guy obviously had little knowledge of *professional* heckling. Rule #1 from *The Heckler's Handbook; Make sure you're heckling from the back of a darkened room, and if they ask your name, say 'Frank.'* If they say, *"Why don't you come up here and say that to my face,"* you say, *"I can't come up there, I'm crippled; maybe NOW you can be funny, you have some cripple jokes, don't you?"* They're left either telling a cripple joke, or just continuing to look stupid, either way, you win. Heckler 1, Comedian 0."

— Lance Hodge

A Small Book of Comedy Publication

Volume 7

Stand-up 6:
The Heckler's Bit

By Lance Hodge

"Hecklers don't get enough credit. Some hecklers spend *hours* preparing their material to attend a comedy show, and then waiting for that *perfect* moment to insert their heckle. I give them a lot of credit, they're up against someone just *waiting* to make them look like a moron; heckling, it's a tough job. But, somebody's got to do it."

-Lance Hodge

Stand-up 6: The Heckler's Bit

By Lance Hodge

Heckling. This is a staple of comedy, comedians get heckled. It's often the new comedian, who gets heckled, who isn't well-known, and hasn't gained some "respect" in the comedy world, or, the very famous comedian, and a heckler who's out to make a name for themselves in the heckling community. As for the non-professional heckler, people like to complain, usually for no good reason. They like to stand out, they crave attention. The comedian must be prepared for the heckler, and have a "Heckler's Bit" ready to go.

A heckler is notoriously easy to defeat. They are often motivated by liquor, low I.Q.'s, being born in Kentucky, a need to 'be noticed,' and by the nightmare of having a tiny penis.

Here are some standard *heckles*.

"You suck."

"You're not funny."

"That's supposed to be a joke?"

"When does your act start?"

"Do you have down's syndrome?"

"I hate you."

"Flies."

"Fuck you."

"Get off the stage."

"Next."

"This isn't comedy."

"You dress funny."

"I haven't laughed *yet*."

"I want my money back."

"Did you know this was a COMEDY club?"

"Amateur."

"Moron."

"Tell a joke."

"I hope they didn't pay you for this."

"Turn off your mic."

The heckler may use *several* of these, or other heckles, and they can be *creative*, so be prepared.

Let me take those standard heckles, and address them one-by-one:

"You suck."

*Suckage is perhaps the **primary** heckle. Here are the top standard comebacks to the "You suck" heckle:*

> "Yes. But only malts, with a straw, not on *dicks*, like you." Or…

> "You should know."

> "Oh yeah?"

> "What did you say?"

> Or…

> "I'm sorry, I was trying to be funny, for YOU, and YOU don't appreciate it. I'm so sorry. Here, here's a better joke, maybe you'll like this one. What did the heckler say that you gave a *shit* about? NOTHING!"

"You're not funny."

This heckle is to be expected, at a comedy show. Here's the #1 comeback:

> "But YOU are. YOU are funny as hell. I'm cracking up here, oh my god, now THAT was a great heckle, it must have taken you hours to work that one out. Would you like to come up here, and do a joke for us? Or another one of your great heckles? Well, if you do, why don't you go fuck yourself instead."

"That's supposed to be a joke?"

This one is easy. You must hit at the essence of the heckler, and hint at his low I.Q.

> "Actually, that joke was amazingly funny. But, it's *risky*, you have to have an I.Q. over 54 to "get it." I'm sorry, I have some low I.Q. jokes coming up soon, and you might like those better."

"When does your act start?"

Using facts will defeat this simple heckle.

> "That's very perceptive of you, and thank you for noticing, *and* keeping track of time like that. My act will start in five seconds. Five, four, three, two, one… "Fuck you.""

"Do you have down's syndrome?"

This heckle is very personal to me. Here's how I handle it.

> "Yes, I *do* have *Down's Syndrome*. I've worked hard to get to this point in my life. I wanted to do better for myself, so I quit my job, as your Shift-Supervisor at McDonald's, and started doing comedy. By the way, your skills at the fryer are awful, you often over cook the fries. Just pull the fucking basket out when the alarm goes off. It's not that hard. And thanks for that question, Frank."

"I hate you."

This heckler gets right to the point. And, it's actually a baseless heckle, since comedians don't care if you hate them, as long as you laugh from time to time.

> "That's ok. Just keep laughing at the jokes. And, while you're at it, stop being an asshole."

"Flies."

This heckle implies that your comedy is "shit," and that it's drawing flies.

> "If you're hinting that my comedy is "shit," well, I just want you to know that if I were to *shit* right here on stage, right now, right here in this spot (and point to a spot) that YOU would come out, and you'd be right *here*, in this spot. (Point to the spot again.) Now that's a *fact*. It's *sickening*, but it's true. As for the "flies" they seem to be coming from this general direction." (And point toward the heckler).

"Fuck you."

I like this heckle. It's doesn't take much to deflect it.

> "No thank you. But thanks for the amazing heckle, it was brilliant, and so original."

"Get off the stage."

This heckler doesn't have much imagination, but at least they aren't vulgar.

> "I *can't* get off the stage. I have a *contract*. And for every *asshole* in the audience, who disrupts the act, I have to stay a minute longer, it's in the contract. So feel free to keep shouting bullshit from back there, I appreciate it."

"Next!"

The heckler doesn't like you, but that's not news to you.

> "You know, when I get off the stage, they'll just bring out *another* comedian, and compared to me, most of them are SHIT. So, if I were you, I'd sit back, have another drink, and maybe re-think that request."

"This isn't comedy."

This heckler is probably NOT an expert on comedy, so you have the advantage here.

> "*Actually*, this IS comedy, but, I'll agree that some comedy is *way* over the heads of people as short as you."

"You dress funny."

The heckler has really blown it here. This is actually a complement to the comedian.

> "Thank you. This is my comedy *uniform*, and it's intended to provoke a heckle, which allows me, early in the act, to say "Fuck you" to someone in the audience, which often gets a rousing round of applause. So thank you. I appreciate that heckle."

"I haven't laughed yet."

You can't please everyone all the time, this heckler has made that clear.

> "I noticed your girlfriend laughing. She has a good sense of humor, that's *obvious*, she's with you."

"I want my money back."

Here's what I'd say.

> "This guy wants his money back. He's upset that spending **twenty bucks** tonight, will mean that now he can't afford that 300-pound transsexual hooker he met just before the show."

"Did you know this was a COMEDY club?"

*This guy is clever. He thinks **he's** a comedian.*

> "Yes sir, I do know this is a comedy club.
> And the manager told me, that one guy had
> snuck in, without paying, and that I should
> be on the look-out for him. He said I'd be
> able to pick him out in the crowd, because
> he'd be the guy sitting alone, sipping vodka
> from a flask, with the smell of puke on his
> shirt. Hey, guy next to him, can you smell
> puke on his shirt? The guy said, "Yes." Ok,
> security, that's your guy."

"Amateur."

*This guy probably goes to comedy clubs frequently. He
probably knows his stuff.*

> "Amateur? Well, you must be an *expert*. Do
> you have a good joke, that I could use? I'd
> really appreciate it. Write it down for me
> OK, on a napkin, and then shove that joke
> up your ass. I'm sure you've had *various*
> things up there."

"Moron."

*Anyone who calls you a moron, is an idiot. Don't forget
that.*

> "Oh, *I'm* a moron. Well, it takes one to
> know one, and I can tell you are NOT a

moron. So that would tend to disprove what you just said. *You're* not a moron, your *mother* is, for not smothering you years ago."

"Tell a joke."

Again, this guy is clever, since that comment makes the audience think you haven't been telling jokes.

> "I planned on telling a joke in just a minute. But first, I have to think of some response to *you*, the mental retard in the audience, who shouts out at the comedian to tell a joke. That's like telling the butcher, at *Vons*, to cut meat. Of course I'll tell a joke, that's what I'm here for, and what the hell are YOU here for? Your mom kicked you off your video games and out of the basement? Probably so she could bring some Johns in tonight, for some extra money. Well, just relax. You can go home soon, if you just shut the fuck up and try not to advertise how stupid you are. Thank you."

"I hope they didn't pay you for this."

*There's a good chance they **didn't** pay you for this, so this might be easy to handle.*

> "No sir, they did not pay me for this. They said they let too many people in tonight that had no money, and were losers, and that they felt sorry for them, and now, they

13

wouldn't be able to pay me anything, because of all the *losers* they let in for free. So no, they didn't pay me, but, I would appreciate a "Thank you."

"Turn off your mic."

This heckler has probably used this line before, he may be a professional heckler.

"Sir, are you a professional heckler? Because you are so *good* at it. I'm impressed. You certainly got some attention with that clever heckle. And I *would* turn off my mic, and just *yell* the rest of the act, if YOU would promise to leave. Do we have a deal?"

The "noise." The heckler makes some loud noise.

This could be the imitation of an animal, a snoring sound, a squeal, scream, or other guffaw. Here's some possible comebacks.

"Wow. THAT was something!"

"Did that guy just speak in tongues?"

"What the hell was that?"

"OK. A man in row 26 was just stabbed, would someone call security."

"Sir, that was just a rat. Relax. It'll scurry away soon, they always do."

So, this is a good start, in case you are an aspiring comedian, and you don't have your own *Heckler's Bit* yet, you can use some of these.

This whole "Comedy thing" is *amazing*, a good comedian is *special*, maybe not 'short bus' special, but *maybe*. A comedian gets paid, sometimes, to observe simple things, and to notice something about those things, something that's odd, or stupid, or surprising, or otherwise unnoticed by everyone else. Some people *do* notice these things, and shake their heads about it, or comment to someone about it, but they don't have the ability to turn it into a *joke*. A comedian has that special talent, they are the *jokey* sort. Some comedians are *brilliant*, in an actual I.Q. sort of way, there are *three* such comedians. Most comedians are misfits, losers, and mental cases, which often makes them even funnier.

This book serves two purposes:

1. Entertainment.
2. Training

Some people simply seek to be *amused*, and they buy a book like this, that promises to *amuse* them. Others, the minority of readers, seek *training* in this mysterious realm of "Comedy."

For the aspiring Comedian, buying a book like this, is the first sign, a tell-tale sign, of *failure*. You can't learn comedy from a *book!* That's like trying to learn to be an engineer, or a doctor, or an English teacher, from a *book*. If you want to be an engineer, or doctor, or English teacher, you just have to go out and do it! *Forget the books*. Want to be an engineer? Go build a bridge from your house to your neighbor's house, that you could drive a car over, just do it! Doctor, go diagnose people; sniffy nose = cold. Fever, *infection…* you get the idea. Want to be an English teacher, first, why? Second, just like engineers and doctors, just start *doing it*, start correcting people's grammar, and spelling; *Facebook* is a great place for this, it will also get rid of some of those "Friends" that you really didn't need anyway. And this advice is the same with comedy, if you want to be a comedian, start telling jokes, make people laugh, get a black t-shirt.

As for heckling, the *Internet* is FULL of information on, and examples of, *heckling*. This is one reason that there are so many hecklers, and how so many of them get so good at it. Actually, *most* aren't that good, the incidence of a "successful" heckler is quite low, but still, even at a 1% **S.H.R.** *(Successful Heckle Rate),* with all the comedy happening out there, that amounts to 137.6 *successful* heckles per year, which, at least for comedians, is 137.6 too many.

The worst thing that can happen to a comedian, is to *fail* at their response to the heckler. Some comedians have, while or after failing at their response to the heckler: *Broken guitars over the head of a heckler, began to cry and then walked off stage, had no, or a very lame response to the heckler*, which means, the heckler "won," which should NEVER be allowed to happen. And *some* comedians, not properly prepared for the heckle, respond in some way that is *wildly* inappropriate, remarkably *offensive*, and will end up on TMZ with Harvey Levin telling everyone that this comedian is a *jerk*, and that his career is over, or should be. Such an expose' on TMZ could be a career killer!

But some comedians, will turn the next ten minutes of their act, following a heckle, into a *hilarious* response to the heckler, causing the heckler to shut up, or even better, to go out and hang themselves from a street light after the show.

So, that's the basics of heckling.

What follows is heckling *science*, for the heckler.

I like to be fair and balanced, so I'll also give the heckler a little advice here. First, I'll just list some of the *rules*, from **The Heckler's Handbook**:

Rule #1

Make sure you're heckling from the back of a darkened room, and if they ask your name, say 'Frank.' If they say, *"Why don't you come up here and say that to my face,"* you say, *"I can't come up there, I'm crippled; maybe NOW you can be funny, you have some cripple jokes, don't you?"* They're left either telling a cripple joke, or just continuing to look stupid, either way, you win. Heckler 1, Comedian 0."

Rule #2

Heckling is a *calling*. The "comedian" is a *jerk*. The "comedian" lives his or her life making fun of people, like you. He or she spends many hours writing down jokes that demean, humiliate, and seek to crush self-esteem, YOUR self-esteem. Don't hold back, hit them hard with your heckle, you are fighting evil.

Rule #3

Prepare, prepare, prepare. That means, prepare *three* times. #1 Prepare *before* you even know what "comedy" show you're going to. #2 Prepare for the *specific* show, and that *specific* "comedian," after you find out what show you're going to. *(Watch YouTube videos of that "comedian;" this will allow you to know what's coming, and when in their show to insert your heckle)* #3 Prepare, *silently*, while standing in line at the show, to get yourself all *psyched up.*

Rule #4

Timing is crucial. When preparing to deliver your heckle, wait for an opening. The comedian will pause, but perhaps only briefly, you must know when to strike! A poorly timed heckle will fail badly, and you'll look stupid.

Rule #5

The heckle must be loud enough to be heard by the "comedian" and by at least a *dozen* of people in the audience. *Annunciate, project, deliver.* This may end on a DVD, or on streaming video, speak up!

Rule #6

Regardless of the "comedian's" response, have your *follow-up heckle* ready, and hit them with it *quickly*. *Never* answer a question from the "comedian," that is *always* a trap.

Rule #7

If you feel that the "comedian" has scored some points with their response, feign a seizure, to gain sympathy, and to stop the onslaught. If the "comedian" makes fun of your fake seizure, bite your tongue, HARD, to cause bleeding, and then cough out some blood. Don't stop seizing, until security drags you out of the venue.

Rule #8

The heckler never loses. Worst case scenario, the audience is laughing at you, you have been ridiculed, and most people think the "comedian" has won; as security drags you out, yell out *"I win."* The "comedian" rarely has a good comeback for *that*. You win!

Rule #9

Get loaded. Alcohol, of course, and add psychoactives, if possible. Avoid *barbiturates*, you need to be on your toes. Hallucinating while heckling *is* advised, there are no downsides to this, it WILL make your heckle MUCH funnier, if not to the audience and the "comedian" then to *you*. Again, no downside here. Mushrooms are your little friends.

Rule #10

The final rule is *never* written down, to avoid potential legal action. But, it includes various "last resort" measures, when your heckling has failed. I'm not saying "stalking" or "false reports to TMZ" or to "child protective services" are part of Rule10, that's up to you, to come up with appropriate *other* "measures" if your heckling has failed.

~

As you can see, heckling has become a science, and hecklers take this *seriously*. The good news, most hecklers are *not* professionals, have *not* read *The Heckler's Handbook*, and are stupid.

My advice to hecklers, *have at it*. You'll usually end up looking like a jerk, and most comedians are ready for you, and may even relish the chance to go mano-a-mano with you. And, in some rare instances, YOU *will* win. The *Comedian* will look like an idiot, and YOU will look like a *genius*. Just like terrorists, when the word gets out, into the *heckler community*, you will be an instant hero. Your photo will be pinned up in the parent's basement of many hecklers, and you may be offered the chance to speak at Heckler's Conventions. So have it!

That's really all there is to heckling. Let's switch tracks here…

I know that many of you have no intention of pursuing a career in comedy, and are reading this for its *comedy* content, to maybe get a *giggle* or two, well, how's that working out?

Let's say you're a comedian, and you've got your *Heckler's Bit* ready; that's a BIG help, and it takes a LOT of pressure off. But now, you need *The First 15-Seconds*. The first 15-seconds is a BIG DEAL. When you walk out on stage, the clock is ticking, the 15-second clock. In that *first 15-seconds* you must GRAB THEM, so to speak. Do NOT actually grab anyone, there are laws covering "battery" that could come into play here. In those first 15-seconds you've got to make them *think* you are about to be *hilarious!* It could be a funny face, some body language, your first words, or *sounds*, or some *physical* comedy.

Physical comedy may include how you enter the stage; fast, slow, haltingly, or how you move the microphone, stool, or water bottle, and of course your physical *appearance*, including clothing.

1. You could walk out on stage in a weird way.
2. You could smile weirdly, or laugh, or whistle, or grunt.
3. You could look up and say something to God.
4. You could touch your crotch.
5. You could stumble, or actually fall.
6. You could try to adjust the microphone, but knock it over instead.
7. You could try to sit on the stool, but fall off.
8. You could have lots of trouble opening your water bottle, or complain that it isn't *Perrier*.
9. You could just be a weird-looking person.
10. You could be dressed funny.

All that and more should be considered when thinking about that first *15-seconds*. As you can see, this whole comedy thing is complex, it takes planning, and deep thought. I forgot #11, you could have a *cowbell* on stage, and begin *whacking it* for the first 15-seconds, that can't fail.

I'm not sure if I'll put some biography on the back cover of this book, but, elsewhere in this series of comedy books, I detailed my *qualifications* to give you comedy advice. Some people who can't *do*, teach. Writing a book like this can certainly be categorized as *teaching*, but I've also *done*. I won't repeat all the details here, but I've been a comedian ALL my life. Most people consider their *birth day* as their beginning, but we were *cooking* before that, and for those last couple of months anyway, we were "us." I've been a comedian since at least *seven months*. I found a LOT of stuff humorous in the *uterus*, and I even formulated some jokes about it. I told several of those jokes, *in* the uterus, to *myself*, and, like *Tom Hanks* in "Castaway" talking to a volleyball, I was also talking to the *uterus*, the *placenta*, and that *umbilical cord*. They weren't as good an audience as *Wilson*, but that's all I had. Anyway, I came up with a pretty good *three-minutes* in the uterus, and I did that three minutes MANY times after I was born, but nobody could understand me, it was a tough crowd.

So I have *experience* here, *plenty* of experience to write a book about comedy. And, I've got some advice on *facial expressions*, but, because of spacing issues in this book, I'll begin that lesson on the next page, since there's not nearly enough room here, at the end of this page, to start it. I'll do what I've done before when faced with this problem, and insert some graphic…

Disturbing graphic: child thrown HARD onto table

So here's the lesson on facial expressions, and how important they can be:

New glasses

Copyright 2013 L. Hodge

New glasses

New glasses

Copyright 2013 L. Hodge

27

New glasses

Copyright 2013 L. Hodge

28

New glasses

Copyright 2013 L. Hodge

It goes without saying, but I'll say it, that *facial expressions* can make or break you in comedy.

This is what we're *shooting for* in a comedy show.. camera pans to woman in audience.

Copyright 2013 L. Hodge

And *this* is a *bad* sign…

Ginger with blue sweater

Since we've moved into art appreciation, here's this.

The guy at the top, that's *Jesus H. Christ*.

~

If you've been reading this little book for *entertainment* purposes, I hope, at the very least, you *smiled*, and if you *chuckled*, all the better. I was going for *mirth*, but a *chuckle* is fine. And, if you *do* try to become a comedian, you'll need an appropriate **exit**.

Try to leave *right* after a *really* good joke, *before* the laughter has died down. Or, if there was no joke, and it isn't funny, and you're bombing really badly, cut your losses, and get the hell out of there.

Grab your water bottle, give em a big smile, and then just say, *"Good night,"* and *go*.

Don't tell them they've been a great audience, that might go to their heads, and, if you've bombed, if they didn't laugh much, it was probably *their* fault, and they were a really *shitty* audience. Just say *"Good night,"* and go.

"Good night."

Cat

The cat is inserted here to remind you that no *pussies* were harmed in the making of this comedy book.

Also, that cat is there as an illustration for this little saying, from Sgt. Cadle, **U.S. Army Drill Sargent:** *"Welcome to Fort Ord you pussies. For the next few months, we are going to turn you pussies into MEN. If you're some sort of comedian, forget that shit here, this isn't funny."*

Turns out, he was wrong, it was funny as hell.

To be continued...

Available at **AMAZON**.com
Other books by Lance Hodge

Stand-up: In Search of One-Hour

Stand-up 2: An Idiot's Guide to Comediocity

Stand-up 3: The Five Steps to being Funny, for the price of four

Stand-up 4: "Now that's funny"

Stand-5: Comedian slash Paramedic

Comedy in 5, 4, 3, 2, 1

The Master Works: Art

Everything you already knew about everything

Christopher Walken reads: The Three Little Pigs

Secrets of my Grandfather: A guide to Life's Wisdom

Dexter Doubletree, Detective Stories

Christopher Walken reads: Where the wild things are

The Master Works: Art 2

AMAZON.com, Booksamillion.com, Barnes

& Noble, and other fine book sellers

.

Made in the USA
Las Vegas, NV
28 February 2022

44758900R00024